A WALK
IN WINTER

SEAN STREET

A WALK
IN WINTER

ENITHARMON PRESS 1989

First published in 1989
by the Enitharmon Press
40 Rushes Road
Petersfield
Hampshire GU32 3BW

ISBN 1 870612 25 6

The Enitharmon Press acknowledges
financial assistance from Southern Arts

Set in 10 point Bembo
and printed by
Strand Press, Petersfield, Hampshire

Cover design by Michael Whittaker

For my parents

CONTENTS

A WALK IN WINTER

It is a path yet to be followed, this broken road —
a cartway seen but not taken all these years,
even unthought of — unworthy of walking
on all but the worst days, when all else fails.

And now the ice digs deep, mud's hard edge
cuts at a stumble to bruise us blue,
but today it is a path to be followed
that the summer you saw, your last season, forsook.

The decaying fact of your absence freezes, stiffens —
holly blooms blood warnings in dishevelled hedges,
but flow and rot are suspended, held by the clamp of cold.
Nothing moves until a puddle cracks and water spills.

And over the hard calm curve of the winter down,
across the field, the lane's clear expectancy, there falls
last light from a sky of unshed snow,
fragile as frost's crisp feather on the rutted track.

FACE

This is the landscape across which
we build dry walls, severing fields.
Rock strives up — this white bone — stitched

under hills' broken curve; age yields,
down where the line collapses, dies,
grows indistinct; watch how dusk builds

conscience heavy over it — skies
for a land shaped by being, all
these stones, these shadows, silent cries. . .

White-bone landscape — down hills, dry walls.

TIME AND PLACE
(Budleigh Salterton)

A rich dark room with its
much-sought Millais beach view —
an old clock counts
audibly, visibly, to and fro.

Outside the steep stone bank
dips in steps to the sea.
It is not easy, lying here, to think
beyond it, beyond the pebbles' floor,

those smooth familiar oval shapes
and the old boat-winch's grind.
But this blank absence gropes
at the air within, while wind

beyond the flexing glass
beats down; men turn back on such nights,
stumbling on shingle, as loose
spray dusts the red cliffs, and lights

flick on in Marine Parade.
Here there is the clock
untouched by the elements, hard,
cloistered, its tapping stick

sewing the time into silence.
The storm shifts, a gull cries,
barometers fall. With a new virulence
the evening's ticking cell multiplies.

MORGAN'S HILL

After the rain
a long view — and larks.
A climb through three gates,
but worth it for the best of Wiltshire.
We, surprised even now by this green antiquity
touching instinct, breathe in and smile.

And the sun points out meadows,
clouds paint themselves
and high Morgan's Hill sings its great wide song
to us until

we turn to the circle of trees,
and the hollow hauls us into itself.
A stump, scattered stones,
a fire's corpse and a stagnant pool;
a rook floats, sodden, swollen.
Here we are no longer part of things —
or part of something other.

We leave symptoms of ourselves everywhere.
Out there the winds dilute us.
Here, face to face with these echoes,
we fall silent.

Saddened, with nothing
but the rushing of beech about us,
we stumble out,
finding a sky we do not recognize
full of something darker than the rain.

WAITING

Stasis — Time like river round a post —
the stretch of the long beam at the dark
door's prizing, this weather of waiting,
the mundane detail too sharp, the day
happening as a series of stills.

Then the next room's lambency enters,
wilfully the facts accelerate,
real light writes itself on water, cold,
suddenly tidal. Old wood rots, falls
as lost flotsam at the swift stream's will.

SIX POSTCARDS

1

Heading South-west

Basingstoke on the right nudges the M3;
left, meadows retreat into trees.
The familiar slow lane rolls through the machine,
bridges ticking overhead, each taking its turn,
sunset waiting as usual at perspective's end.

Then without warning something unseen overtakes,
Time's caught and passed by a headlong memory
driving out of a day you never knew
to where, alive, you never went,
finding you everywhere, always.

2

Rain, Southampton

In the end, after all that we've been,
our long days collect for me
in one image, lights captured through
an inverted luminosity;
Town and Water — a colloquy.

But now where is your memory?
Split halves of a glass shattered
by false reality: who echoed whom?
Two mirrors — just as if it mattered...
just as if it mattered.

3

Knowlton, Cranborne Chase

The fallen church deconsecrates
forgotten ritual with a broken cross.
Something shared bridges millennia —
ruin within ruin, one wrecking the other.

From all around the ghosts come to die,
hanging leafy heads, drifting in
from Badbury and Ackling Dyke —
relics over which their congress broods.

It is not strange that the hill turns away,
refusing our further persuasions,
for it has renounced its own phantoms,
thrown all past life to Win Green's winds.

4

Out of Season, Bournemouth

Out in the bay, the ghost
of a launch plugs
across still, fogged sea.
Necrosis settles over skin,
a feeble tide licks at its own garbage —
weed, a plastic bottle, oil smears.
The lapping waves have no heart
to rinse the bowl tonight.
The last of the season drains,
the launch leaves a pause instead of a wake.

5

Mason, Wimborne Minster

Wall and the shaping scar
part and inseparable, the how
and what gone and unlooked for,
but crucial from then to now.

Earth has exchanged its bone
for a hand, a balance restored,
supporting soil and this stone,
knowing both last, durable, hard.

6

Bucklers Hard

Walk in any road, on any path, there is the salty taste
of living lingering on earth's tongue —
world a merchant's yard, full of crash and shout,
the savoury essence of hands' work,
life's job being done, going on continually.

So the shipwright and carpenter, farmer and clerk
with tool and thought hold themselves up to time,
printing a being on future years,
a richness that colours light parchment.
Even in silence the air is left ringing.

MONDAY

Hard rain across an inverted morning,
a scrap of silver paper flickers on the path,
slippery light slides by overhead.
On such days we notice detail:
the head hangs, eyes seek harder.

A dawn that won't be dragged from dusk,
and litter, the day's first vortex.
For us, reflection is brighter than image,
so Monday puts the onus on our inner warmth,
but place informs attitudes, and rain's a cruel accomplice.

POEM AT AVEBURY

I circumnavigate the ring,
and one by one the stones strive to speak,
their incomprehensible language
smoothed to a rough muffled grunt
by the unimaginable years.

There ought to be a poem in them,
a metaphor to prize out,
a song carved into their bodies —
even an enigma would be enough!

But until the stone in me
shall be revealed, I shall not know it.

Every poem grows out of such soil,
out of questions, out of the dark . . .
but not at Avebury.
Here, the fact of place negates all words.

The green waves roll in,
sheep in the dusk glimmer like sarsens.

Nothing to write of here.
The stones are their own poem —
a poem must be its own man, after all.

FLINT WITH SEAWEED

Rain, darkness very close.
A wisp of hair, a chalice of bone
facing the broken sea blind-eyed.
A profile pecked at by gulls,
spiked for the grey winds' peeling, cleansing.

Shape made image — pluvial or marine,
carved into significance by mood and circumstance —
once, stone with a smear of congealed fungus,
now a likeness cast from spring seas' solstice,
stinging with meaning and salt.

The tide sifts — in the end
all ends where it should —
weed pulled by waters, the flint drowning.
A squall cuts, the sea sucks . . .
All to our own homes, each in his separate night.

CHURCHYARD YEWS

Even on the good days
we are brought back by these avenues —
gravel paths, white stones,
deceptively decorative in morning light.

Like blue-black sermons, foliate Bibles,
they are tidy, we prize them,
pretending we have control,
imagining them to be trees.

Their image rhymes with grief,
respect, but no sympathy;
winter clings perennially,
feeding, feeding downwards.

Flames burn darkly out of soil
half-flesh by now.
Their timeless sombre tact
is an understanding that ought to be mutual. . .

It remains a metaphor we cannot quite grasp,
or is it that Death breeds them,
roots in the unthinkable ground
foliage stopping the sunlight short?

Confetti-bells flower the springtime light,
the font spills its ancient holy fruit;
Yews await their day in silence —
they are their own shadows, they become ours.

FOG — WEST WIGHT

For Brian Hinton

Last night, the sea turned to smoke and flooded;
it spilled up the cliff,
brimming over, drowning house and garden
in a gasp of grey.

From deep, deep beneath its waves,
strange monstrous moon-eyed fish moaned,
a low hooting,
their cries the texture of sad wool.

Now nothing else lives.
From Wight the tide spreads out,
and we on a new ocean bed see an end
to the drenched world in its whispering caul.

BIRD IN A CHURCH

There were white walls, there was invocation,
and out of the sun, fire came flying,
a second's sharp miraculous blaze
there on a candlestick, a flickering
to kindle the altar's purple torch.
At the turn of a full eye, vision
before the cerebrum's damp prose,
this flash through the stone dusk;
how the prayers burned,
how the dark flame fluttered!

DRIVING HOME FROM CRANBORNE

Out of the lane's wood, a bare winter tunnel, through
and up, driving towards the wide fields' curved plateau,
but seeing first only sky where the road glows blue . . .

and Old Man's Beard furring every hedge and tree
like frost, while at four the real frost forms around me —
over the Chase, light bleaching to beige, emptily.

Up, up and out of the arms of houses to where
the distance rains in from all sides, open, clean, spare —
pointed at sunset, one flamingo cloud, like hair.

Behind, Church and Manor settling into the dusk
together, clutched under beeches — no more to ask
of the day now but this engine's chore, this road's task.

BEACH BUILDING

On the winter shore they are remaking what years have undone.
While the grey light surges in over horizon's hill,
they push a wedge into the sea — stone, wood — a groyne
through sand and shingle, a fence against salt water's will.

The litter of August, an inhabited promenade, are unimaginable today;
the blank cliff rings back as a pile drives down.
Undressed and empty, the tired resort gives way
to cold rain; behind the front, just another bleached-out town.

With giant stabs from sinking machines, men fight the incoming tide.
Long ago this place invented sand's presence as its reason for being,
and the longshore striving must at all costs be stayed
against the drift's advocacy, the waves' oblique instinct of freeing.

Here through the soft shale they have been vainly making
sheep-pens for distant fictions — carved in January, bulwarks
to hold summer fantasies — but the walls keep breaking.
Down on the winter shore, spring tides stalk our strongest works.

NOVEMBER, 5.30 a.m.

Winter, cold against the glass, stares in,
a part of the night's long empty room,
unlooked for as something forgotten, then gone
strangely, with the light's first bloom.

A part of the night's long empty room,
this jagged pre-dawn ghost stops and looks
strangely, with the light's first bloom
around it, essence a fact that shocks.

This jagged pre-dawn ghost stops and looks,
and I look back, blank, not seeing
around it essence, a fact that shocks:
I see only intrusion, alien being.

And I look back, blank, not seeing.
New time, ice-clad, etches glass,
I see only intrusion, alien being
feel change attack the lonely house.

New time, ice-clad, etches glass
unlooked for as something forgotten, then gone.
Feel change attack the lonely house —
Winter, cold against the glass, stares in.

WHITE WOOL

1

The confluence of valleys drew the eye,
required us to relive the place,
and so we did, you for the shape the fields
delineated, I for the close particularity of flint,
though we were shaped by both.

Here is so much more than memory,
the encountering of winters
through the endless years
for a life strong as a yoke, broken like a butterfly.
The changing shadows, new fields appearing, fading
new men appearing, fading. . .
The valley speaks in us, even now.
Something genetic caught in the soil's rubble —
chip and break of stone,
of bone, of lives lived — made us.

2

Up here with the larks
the air is clear across to a distant down
but Old Winchester Hill turns over and sleeps.
This is beauty, yes, but this is a place
where men lived, part of the beauty
and alive to the need to live
with the plough that choked on flint,
the furrow carved by the fear of the crop that fails. . .
a long past of trying,
as much here as anywhere.

These fields hold the dialect of it all
as they pour down to Meon,
shaped by tackle and a long day
till dusk, and light in the white house door.

And now the gate rusts fast.
The path is lost in the corn
and the old voices fade.
But the house is there, a shout
in the valley to echo under the copse,
a great white cry, white as the ancient wool,
and the hill-top road does not change.

3

Do not be seduced by beauty.
Life is hard here too —
we are witnesses to that. Years lived
in the shadow of this hill, lives lived
in the shadow of these years.
Old Winchester Hill sleeps on,
White Wool works on through flint and furrow
carving Meon Valley, shaping the voices,
the conduct of men.

And monks in the vineyard saw it,
men on the old downs,
the harvester that hums under the hill's crest...
The mirror holds the image of the dead man —
there are voices, faded, but one upon another, singing,
heard in the very contours of the ground.
We hear them, we perceive them,
you in the shape the fields delineate,
I in the close particularity of flint;
we two shaped by both belong here.

NOTHING'S CHANGED

"Nothing's changed," you said, and I could see
that nothing had. . . We journeyed back towards
your infancy — child and parent — studied closely
the algebra of family. Out of all this came the life
that since, for you, has happened. And now I'll travel
back alone, perhaps in spring; for May it was
that we were there, and I shall come to see, like you,
that nothing's changed, and everything at once.

FIRE-BREAK, FEBRUARY

Landscape ecru, and under its mood
a composition of shades
that unifies earth and sky
from hard rut to unborn snow —
where somewhere close, deer,
buff and dapple, tremble
in a blending wash,
a season's weathering.
But the first image is mud, tangle,
is unredeemable wreckage,
forest an unkept yard,
nothing a brain can lend structure.

To attempt here a bare foot
on cold bracken, to look for such as
the wood — essence of tree — to unencumber perception
would be to take it on its own terms,
reflect in more than an eye,
then feel soil loosen under frost
as fact, without subjection to hope's metaphor,
without refraction of light. . . .
Stillness the consistency of undyed linen,
a composition of shades
that unifies before change — the relax of earth
or snow's quiet deception — happens.

BODMIN MOOR

Over webs of dry stone
the frantic burning of stars
illuminates nothing —
an unembellished night
astringent with fact.

So a search for new reasons;
understanding the landscape's metaphor,
earth's every wound and sublimity teaching
degree of worth immaterial:
being, the only excellence.

STARLINGS

Winter sycamores grow black leaves —
starlings, massed against dusk — thousands
filling the frosting air with sound
and the bare branches with oiled wings.

A sudden silence and swooping,
for they must hear signals we miss. . .
time, frost, tide — something has brought them
to these trees, to this growing dark.

AUTUMN

The gale brought autumn —
leaves and the trees' weak limbs
fell then — and the sun
abandoned us. We sang hymns
to God, but no one
lived in hope, and the storm won,
colours shift to dun,
we paid for sins.

I recall how we once drank deep,
mourning a lost light,
the life gone to sleep,
gone back to the long night.
But it made me weep,
you giving up the fight
too. You said life is cheap,
and I said, it's your right.

OCTOBER 12th

All year it has been there, though hidden well,
looking like all the other numbers, just
waiting to be ticked with barely a glance,
a date to pass through, as we thought we must.

And yet now, see what it has done to us?
Just see what, all the time, it held in store:
a day to trip us, through remaining years.
How could we not have noticed it before?

THE LEAVES ARE DOWN

The leaves are down from all but the cherry now.
The lawn grows autumn toadstools, fog falls, a frost,
the dark house gapes, the clocks go back, but
the cherry holds its leaves, refusing to believe in winter
even now.

WINDFALLS

A final gift — you gave me pears,
fruit from your autumn grass.
There they are today, ripe and sweet,
storm's consolation, a third day's harvest.

WHITCOMBE CHURCH

February 15th,1885: *"Father was driven over to Whitcombe and took the last service he was able to take. In the same little church in which his ministry began, there he ended it."*

Laura, daughter of William Barnes

(The church is no longer used for regular worship)

He has become light.
The redundant cross holds the image,
a picture on a dead eye.

First and last words and all between
are here; the sounds, though silent, stay.

Over the hill and back they took him,
through the field and winter trees,
and he knew, because wise in humanity,
that soon it would be time,

time to be part of it all at last, to feel
a budding from experience to being.

And here, where a last prayer hung,
he has become light —

the signals persist —

I see him. . . he touches me.

NOW

When friends ask, I go through it all again —
an autopsy on love, knowing now where to begin
where once I was wordless through obsequies
and the sharp recollection of lost intimacies.

Now the body, bound up with memory,
seems to hold its reality quite well, and I'm ready
for questions, can make a show of whether
I was right, and how and why, piecing it together.

So I go on digging my own sweet grave,
an Egyptian throwing in loved artefacts I've saved.
I rouge the dead cheeks, falsify the end;
once I was alive and wordless, now I can pretend.